10 STEPS TO RECLAIM EUROPE

Programme for the European Right

By Drieu Godefridi

© Texquis, November 2018
ISBN 978-2-930650-20-3

SUMMARY

Introduction: The disagreement between optimists and pessimists 5

1. Illegal immigrants 7
2. Family reunification 11
3. "European law" 15
4. Assimilation 19
5. Public expenditure 23
6. Accountability of the "magistrates" 27
7. Pluralism 29
8. ECHR 33
9. Maghreb 37
10. Civilization 39

Conclusion: Ten steps to reclaim Europe 45

Introduction: The disagreement between optimists and pessimists

Among those who are interested in the future of our continent and, more generally, of our civilization, two distinct trends have emerged.

Firstly, the optimists. They are those who point out that our standard of living has never been higher, that technological progress is rampant, that hunger in the world is declining, that fewer and fewer wars are being fought, and so on. Undeniable truths held dear by classical-liberals.

Then, there are the pessimists, looking for indications and signs of the impending fall of our civilization: demographic collapse, migratory anarchy, ever-heavier taxation, the loss of common cultural reference, etc. Matters as undeniable as those highlighted by our optimists!

So, who should we side with? Quite frankly, with neither. While the standpoints of optimism and pessimism are not without merit, they are in fact of limited intellectual interest and of no functional value.

These stances are not without precedent. Pessimism and optimism reigned in equal parts in the early thirties, when both the Left and the Right professed that never again would the Germans venture to conquer Europe. But by the time Winston Churchill became prime minister in 1940, the overwhelming majority in both Britain and Europe were very much resigned to the final, inevitable and definitive victory of Nazism.

What did Churchill do? A simple calculation of the opposing forces involved. The Churchillian calculation was simple, considering only two factors: men and industrial power. If the United States were not to declare war, Churchill stated, Germany would defeat and impose its domination on a significant fraction of the world. Yet if the formidable industrial capacity of the Americans, and their significant reserves of men were to come to the front, Germany would be defeated.[1]

What can we learn from this? Pessimism and optimism are only of limited interest. Consider only the calculation of the primary forces involved, and how best to engage in a pro-active approach.

I would like to propose ten steps, if I may, to save Europe.

Here limited to a mere ten though, admittedly, the list could have increased by a dozen other steps. It seemed preferable to cut to the essential, focusing on the main factors influencing the future of the European continent: Law; tax; migration; effective pluralism in the press, the judiciary and education; and above all culture.

For the *war of the gods* – to quote Max Weber[2] — of which we are now witnesses and actors, it is not primarily political or intellectual; it is deep and visceral, touching the very foundations of our civilization. This war of the gods is, to borrow from Bismarck, a *Kulturkampf*; a cultural war between two radically irreconcilable value systems: the system of freedom, which underpins our civilization, and that of socialist egalitarianism.

---

[1] "We had won the war": W. Churchill, December 8, 1941. *The Second World War*, vol. III, chapter 32.

[2] "As long as life has a meaning in itself and it understands itself, it knows only the eternal conflict that the gods wage between themselves or, moving away from the metaphor, it knows only that the incompatibility of ultimately possible points of view, the impossibility of settling their conflicts and, consequently, the necessity of deciding in favour of one or the other": Max Weber, *The Vocation Lectures*, Paris.

1. Illegal immigrants

It is always amusing to hear a politician or NGO arguing for the rule of law yet, in the same breath, furiously opposing the arrest and expulsion of clandestine immigrants. For it is unquestionable, however, that every such illegal immigrant represents the contradiction of democracy and the rule of law.

The facility of legal migration to Europe has never been so developed and "generous" — for the newcomers — in our history, and is the most open and "humanitarian" in the world.

Yet there are millions of migrants who do not satisfy the conditions, no matter how slight they might be, who decide nevertheless to migrate to Europe, in fraudulent and categorical violation of its laws.[3]

---

[3] Estimates regarding illegal immigration widely vary. Euronews, citing Eurostat, estimated that there were 618,780 illegal immigrants in Europe in 2017 ("last year, 618,780 non-EU citizens were illegally present in the EU": https://www.euronews.com/ 2018/07/09 / number-of-illegal-immigrants-in-eu-decreases-while-number-of-those-kicked-out-rise). On September 29, 2017, however, the European Commission announced its intention to repatriate 1.5 million illegal immigrants (https://www.lemonde.fr/europe/article/2017/09/27/ bruxelles-veut-accelerer-le-retour-de -1-5-million-to-migrants-illegaux_5192251_3214.html). That's more than double. How can one reconcile these two figures? In fact, Euronews quotes Eurostat incorrectly. 618,780 is the number of illegal immigrants identified in 2017 in European territory by the authorities. This number was 983,860 in 2016, and 2,154,675 in 2015. Therefore, Euronews cites as a total what is only the number for a single year. Moreover, these "identifications" concern only certain clandestine immigrants, some of them escaping any form of control and identification thanks to their classification. It is therefore impossible to produce a precise figure. The annual number of identifications of illegal immigrants has been around 500,000 (still according to Eurostats), with the peaks indicated, the total number is probably about 10 to 15 million illegal immigrants. In the United States, for comparison, the Pew Institute estimated in 2017 the number of illegal immigrants to 11 million.

These laws, don't forget, embody not only European and national legality, but they are also the result of parliamentary majorities.

That such laws are violated is human, "normal" in the sense of Durkheim.[4] But to encourage their violation, to demand that this delinquency in the strict sense of the word, persists without consequence, amounts to substituting the rule of the mob for the rule of law and democracy. The intelligentsia presenting the violation of our laws as morally superior to their application is a farce.

"Easier said than done" is the parting shot of those who concede the rational argument. We would like to, but in practice it is impossible: an argument recently forwarded by the President of the German Parliament Wolfgang Schaüble.

Nothing could be further from the truth. Collective expulsions would simply require the meeting of two preconditions.

First, neutralize the European Court of Human Rights (ECHR). Blinded by its own extremist creed, the ECHR renders and will render impossible any rational and moderate policy of return to democracy and the rule of law as regards migration. Countries that want to regain control of their borders will have to secede from the human rights convention to preserve their national sovereignty (we will come back to this).

Next to be considered is tangible cooperation with the Maghreb countries, from which comes — directly or in transit — the overwhelming majority of those illicitly in Europe. This necessitates a return to power politics: the Maghreb depends on Europe economically. It may be largely unvoiced yet it is a geopolitical truism.

---

[4] Émile Durkheim, "On the normality of crime", 1895.

Therefore, Europe is entitled to expect the cooperation of these countries regarding migration, and to reduce its trade with and aid to any such country that would refuse frank and fair cooperation.

The expulsion of the millions of illegal immigrants present on European soil entails neither violence nor inhumanity, only the return to democracy and the rule of law. It is the current situation that engenders violence and enables the criminal networks trafficking people to Europe.

Step 1: Effective expulsion of the millions of illegal immigrants present on European soil, as their presence is the negation of democracy and the rule of law.

2. Family reunification

It is customary, when dealing with topics such as the reuniting of families, to say that the institution is noble in principle and that it is the methods of application that are lacking. Then the debate is lost, because how can one affront Morality itself with simple practical considerations.

Family reunification, that is to say the right granted by Western Europeans for an immigrant to bring his family as a whole to Europe, is neither noble nor ignoble in principle. It a response to a mixture of ideological and practical considerations. It is something civilization was able to live without from the Ancient Greeks until the seventies, and was not condemned for doing such.

The trouble is that family reunification has become the main gateway to Europe for millions of immigrants, tagging along behind the "primary" entrants.[5] Each of whom once settled will have the right to bring up to eight people from his or her family — the number varies according to country and legislation. Definitely noteworthy considering Mrs Merkel let about 1.5 million "migrants" come into her territory over a two-year period.

---

[5] In 2015, 45% of the 260,829 visas awarded by Belgium were based on family reunification: http://www.vivreenbelgique.be/11-vivre-ensemble/history-of-immigration-in-belgium-to-look-for-political-led. In 2016, France welcomed 256,000 migrants; mainly due to family reunification: https://www.lesechos.fr/29/06/2017/lesechos.fr/030417560290_la-france--cn-theme-destination-des-migrants.htm. In its 2018 report on migration prospects, the OECD stated that in 2017, family reunification accounted for 40% of migration cases to OECD countries: https: //read.oecd -ilibrary.org/social-issues-migration-health/international-migration-outlook-2018/summary/french_9fe5b4b8-fr#page1

For a million "recognized" primary immigrants, an additional 5, 6 or 7 million immigrants are granted the theoretical right[6] to enter Europe through the magic of "family reunification". The brakes applied to calm popular "worries" — as is the case in Germany — are derisory as long as the *right* to family reunification persists.

Initially a matter of national initiative, family reunification was soon "seized" by the leftist-dominated European Court of Human Rights (ECHR) which rushed to make it a "positive obligation" for Member States (Sen, 2001), and shortly thereafter it was consecrated as a "right" by Directive 2003/86/EC on the right to family reunification, which prohibits member states from the Council of Europe from not practicing family reunification.

Belgium, never slow off the mark regarding immigration, granted, for a while, the right to bring not only spouses and children, but the ascendants too: their parents! Often elderly and in poor health, they were guaranteed access to Belgian Social Security and to the most advanced healthcare available, having of course never contributed a single cent to the system. Even the Belgian legislator had to face the facts, this system was not tenable, and to about-face.

Immigration is the great issue of our time. A country without borders is a contradiction in terms. This is not a subjective opinion: since 2015, most elections in the West have dwelt on the theme of immigration, often on this theme alone, as was the case of the last legislative elections in Hungary and the Czech Republic.

---

[6] Though all will not exercise it its beneficiaries will, in turn, have the right to "family reunification", in an endless chain that the American Right justifiably qualifies as "chain migration".

2. Family reunification

Western Europe has for half a century welcomed tens of millions of immigrants of all origins, including a significant proportion of Muslims, over an extremely short period of time. The public believes that this immigration must be, at least, reduced, to return to an extent which can actually be assimilated.

This return to manageable volumes will not be achieved only at the borders, or through the expulsion of illegal immigrants: it requires the suppression of family reunification, the driving force of mass migration.

Of course, exceptional cases do arise. We do not legislate on the exception.

Step 2: Repeal the right to family reunification.

3. "European law"

It is amusing to see the propensity of some right-wing analysts to argue that the woes of (Western) Europe are the sole fault of the foreigner.

Is this not contradictory with the point of view that has just been implicitly presented? Why then the focus on family reunification and illegal immigrants?

Certainly, but the source of this anarchy is neither African nor Asian. It lies in Europe. It is the European Union and its Court, it is the ECHR — which depends on the Council of Europe and not the EU — and one hundred national initiatives that have created migratory anarchy in Europe. No external power imposed it on us!

That we are the architects of our own tribulations is illustrated by a subject less visible and controversial than migration, but just as influential for our collective future: the proliferation of regulation or *inflation legislative* as the French say.

The European Union originally aimed, at least in its economic aspect (1957), to bring the people of Europe together by weaving trade ties between them. It is not by chance that before being pompously baptized "The European Union", this international organization was more modestly dubbed "The European Economic Community" (widely known as "the common market").

A common market: a simple idea, modest in effect, intended to bring Europeans together, by increasing their collective wealth.

All this was too simple, too empirical and probably too effective for the French mind; they almost immediately commenced the grafting onto the common market of "common policies" which were utterly alien to it. Thus, the famous common agricultural policy, unaffordable, deleterious in its effects, the perfect negation of a free market and the main reason for discord in our commercial relations with our American partners.

The "constructivists" (in the sense of F.A. Hayek) did not stop there: they soon demanded that Europe be made "social" — Jacques Delors! — then "ecological". This is how we began to set in motion and then spur on a gigantic machine — Commission / Parliament / Council – spewing forth regulation.

While preparing for a previous text, it came to mind to assess the exact extent of European regulation. I submitted a freedom of information request which provided the answer to the question: "the edition of the secondary legislation (...) published at the time of the accession of Croatia in 2013 included 16,391 documents (154,834 pages) in 475 volumes."

155,000 pages! The sheer enormity of this mile-high tower of regulation is better measured if one remembers that the Civil Code, which has been a benchmark of governance for two centuries, is entirely contained in a few dozen pages. A few dozen!

Concerning regulation, Americans do show greater political maturity. They readily understand that every rule and paragraph limits freedom and bears an economic cost.

In other words, the basic need for the sound regulation of trade aside, any ruling hinders freedom and economic activity.

The European normative continent, in constant expansion, thus appears as a tectonic anti-economic force intent upon liberticide.

3. "European law"

Let's consider in detail these "regulations". There is no legal text, law, decree or regulation, as antiquated as it may be, which cannot be understood at the first reading, from the *graphē paranómōn* of the Ancient Athenians, to American Tort Law, through to the Civil Code. Not one. Except European law.

Whether in the field of VAT, energy or whatsoever the European bureaucracy spews forth legislation that cannot be understood even at the fifteenth reading. This is due to the often mathematical complexity of the text — an exponential proliferation of mathematical and even chemical equations! in Law! — and self-referential recursion. Not content to discharge regulation continuously, the European Legislator constantly refers back to its previous decrees.

Of course, every article of legislation is a collective work. So much so that their authors are themselves unable to control in their entirety even one Regulation, one Directive.

Saving Europe means ending this madness. This can be envisioned in two ways. Firstly, the revolutionary, tearing down the EU as it stands today. This is not the optimal solution, and we must, from a "Burkean" perspective and bearing in mind Isaiah Berlin's warning against "final solutions" to complex problems, refrain from such action, though understandable the urge may be.

The other way to reduce so-called European "Law" to its most human expression, would be to prune everything that does not belong to the common market. In short, to return to a Europe, which worked for our people and whose added-value was constant, real and essential.[7]

---

[7] This requires, for example, the outright abrogation of the ideological limitations regarding energy, which have led to an enormous hike in the energy bills of households and businesses, significantly contributing to the deindustrialisation of Europe.

It is a well-established misconception that the European Legislator would be unable to tackle the supposedly insurmountable task. Yet it took only four months for four elite jurists to draft the Civil Code, an elegant melange of Roman law and, to a lesser degree, medieval law, overturning millions of local and contradictory laws and customs.

Step 3: Abrogation by a *transcendent synthesis* (Portalis, Hegel) of all that in European "Law" which does not belong to the common market in the strictest sense.

4. Assimilation

Not all foreigners legally present in Europe are Muslims. However, the vast majority of the recent waves of migrants are Islamic[8] and Islam has dogmatic regulation, the only one that claims to compete with Western culture. It is therefore Islam that will be discussed next.

There are many ways to look at the issue of Islam in Europe, most of them flawed.

To treat Islam as a race – and thus reject discussion as racism — is nonsense, yet very popular among leftists. Islam is not a race. There are Muslims of all kinds, origins, races, ethnicities and so forth: Islam in no way regards itself as a race but rather as having a universal vocation and proclaims itself to be the only true religion to which everyone must adhere!

Stating Islam is a religion like any other is another categorical mistake. No, Islam is not a religion like Christianity. With the Quran, Sunnah and Fiqh: Islam is a complete doctrine, intended to utterly govern all aspects of human activity.

Offering itself as an overarching Law and "complete", Islam is contradictory to the idea of the separation of religion and state just as it is to the notion of democracy. Because democracy — the idea

---

[8] While there are accurate ethnic and religious statistics in the United States, there is no such thing in Europe, often for legal reasons. According to the estimates of the "Pew Research Center" there was in mid-2016 in the 28-strong EU plus Norway and Switzerland 25.8 million Muslims. This estimate does not include illegal immigrants or refugees whose asylum claims are under consideration: http://www.pewforum.org/2017/11/29/europes-growing-muslim-population/

that the law is accessible, debatable and definitively amendable by a parliamentary majority — is radically irreconcilable with the idea of an integrated dogma and Law whose seat is divine.

Islam is not a race, Islam is more than a religion. So, how to approach it?

The best way to think of Islam, it seems to us, those best able to be dispassionate in the debate, is to conceive a *political doctrine* (in the broadest sense of the term, such as socialism or liberalism) embodied in a Law that claims to be divine, originating from the supreme being. Such is Islam.

This concept is the most apt in practice. For there is no need to enter into racial or religious considerations to ascertain a historical fact: Islam is a strong and ambitious dogma. Strong because it's underpinned by divinity. Ambitious because, well... just open a history book or an atlas.

Consider the end times of the Classical Era, this period of our history so masterfully portrayed by Henri Pirenne. A Europe caught between the Scandinavian incursions in the North, and the unstoppable Arab-Muslim expansion in the South. A tsunami of Arabic Muslim armies surging from Mecca to Spain and France in a few decades shattered the economic unity of the Mediterranean basin, in place since the Punic wars, and plunged Europe into economic chaos, immediately followed by demographic collapse.

We must read Pirenne who describes those remnants of the European populations who, in Nîmes for example, sought shelter in the Roman arena, using its walls as ramparts to their "city"! Beyond their walls there was only misery and desolation.

If one considers only the legislative level one will note the most striking of contrasts. The Scandinavians, like the Germans before them, almost immediately give up their law and even their language as soon as they come into contact with a law and a civilization whose superiority and practical convenience (most notably juridically) they recognized, namely the Greco-Roman civilization.

When, three centuries later, the Normans invaded England, the masses though Scandinavian turned to the French language and literally *nothing* of their original culture and normativity remained — except the spirit of adventure and an infernal aptitude to crush, often in the most cruel way, anyone who stood in their way.

Quite the opposite in the South. The Arab-Muslim invader took it by force of arms, giving no quarter to its culture nor its law. The Arabic language was universally imposed, and Islamic Law dominated, going so far as to dictate the status — always inferior — of the conquered peoples and their customs.

This imperialism, not only of armies, but of Islamic dogma is historical fact, evident from Spain to the far reaches of the East.

There will be no "fusion" or reconciliation of Islamic and Western dogmas. For, with only the scantest of exceptions, Islam has never acclimated to such reconciliation. And because, most of all, these two dogmas are conceptually irreconcilable. Western Law is based on freedom and presupposes progress (Roman law, common law, democracy). Islamic Law is a divine *logos* that forbids evolution. These two dogmas are conceptually irreconcilable; one or the other will prevail. There will be no middle ground agreed upon.

The whole debate on Islam is distorted by the focus — albeit legitimate — on those most bloodthirsty suras and hadiths of Islamic theology. There is no need to establish a hierarchy between Islamic and Western dogmas to find their incompatibility.

This is why the question of the effective assimilation of those adhering to Islamic culture is critical. Western Europe — as there are hardly any Muslims in most Central European countries — has to stop mistreating itself.

If we want to escape the violence inherent in the confrontation of two irreconcilable belief/legal systems, we must 1) assert the effective protection of the law to any Muslim who wishes to renounce this doctrine and 2) draft a European Islamic Code which reaffirms the absolute accessibility of the Law while countering each and every one of the tenets of Islamic law — Quran, Sunnah, Fiqh — which is irreconcilable in principle (democratic) and / or its substance (equality between men and women, rights of homosexuals etc.) with Western civilization[9].

This will not be painless, it will not be easy. But a deliberate and determined policy, thoughtful and carefully implemented, is better than violence.

Step 4: Adopt a European Islamic Code which reaffirms the absolute accessibility of the Law and counters each and every one of the norms of Islamic law — Quran, Sunnah, Fiqh — which are irreconcilable, in principle or substance, with Western democratic civilization.

---

[9] This European Islamic Code is radically different from the idea of building a "European Islam". If Islam is European it is no longer Islam; if it remains Islam, it is not European. The objective of this European Islamic Code would be more modest: to express the incompatibility of certain Islamic principles and prescriptions with European constitutional legality, in order to render them null and void. Concerning principles and prescriptions that claim to be divine, the approach is justified. Moreover, no real debate on a spirituality that would be European and whose substrate is of Islamic inspiration - among other sources, such as Christianity – shall ever develop, if the terms are not fastidiously posed.

5. Public expenditure

Even though it is convenient to blame others for our misfortunes — Islam, foreign powers etc — it is more enlightening to acknowledge our failings.

It appears that the core problems our societies face is in no way "exogenous" or external, nor the fruit of some curse that may have been cast upon us and of which we are entirely victims, not authors.

This problem is the *socialization* of Europe, a term which can be misleading. Indeed, it has a dual meaning: on the one hand, the process by which a child comes to terms with society; on the other hand, collectivization. In German, they are differentiated nicely — *Sozialisation und Sozialisierung* — something sadly lacking in English or French.

This is regrettable, because the word collectivization, if it is appropriate, smacks of the "USSR" and old-fashioned communism. Nonetheless, in the rest of this text, by "socialization" we will be referring to collectivization in the most literal sense, without any particular historical or doctrinal connotations.

This socialization/collectivization is achieved by taxation, by the Law and finally by ethics.

Taxes are obvious, though do not be fooled by such authors as Thomas Piketty who show that the marginal tax rate was higher in the past than it is today. For, though it be true, in the past some Western countries did experience marginal rates of 80% and even 90%. Yet since 1945, uncharacteristic anomalies aside, taxation in all its forms has continued to grow.

However, this rate does not speak for itself, because you must always look at the rate and the tax *base*. A marginal rate of 55%, levied above 40,000 euros of income, carries a higher *overall* tax burden than a marginal rate of 90%, which only applies above a million euros!

Never has the tax burden been so high in countries such as France and Belgium. Never!

This progression of an intentionally confiscatory tax was one of the measures advocated by the *Communist Party Manifesto* of Marx and Engels; this is the reality we live with — unprecedented socialization/collectivization. Because taxation only equates to spending: the state is not a great saver. Simply put, *the higher the tax, the more effective the socialization.*

Then comes socialization by the Law. We have heard something about European law, regarding its monstrous growth spurred on by the EU's pride in being social, migratory, ecological. But even the EU pales when compared with the runaway burgeoning regulation of certain of its member states.

Belgium for example, only a small country, produces no less than 100,000 pages of *additional* legislation per year! According to our estimates, France produces *every year* as much legislation as it had adopted in the 500 years before the revolution. It is not uncommon for France to adopt a law lengthier, in its own right, than the entire Civil Code.

Thus is the magnitude of the problem.

This Law is "liberal" only in the wildest delusions of those French intellectuals who have lost all contact with reality. It is the second instrument of the socialization of Europe, subjugating and regulating even the smallest detail — a look, a word, an abstention! – of the populace's private lives.

Each law acts to limit, to further restrict that besieged "freedom", ultimately reducing it to nothing. This is a paradoxical era that continues to expand the scope of "human rights", while emptying them of their substance. Because human rights without freedom is a contradiction in terms.

So, the Law and taxation are two matrices of the inexorable socialization of Europe.

Thomas Piketty has shown that one can achieve the goals of communism by circuitous means: that if "high" incomes are sufficiently taxed, they will eventually disappear, without the need to proscribe them.

The same is true of freedom. *There is no need to proscribe freedom in principle, if we remove each of its applications.*

None of this would have been possible if socialism hadn't seized control of the moral high ground. Socialization is possible and widely accepted only if it is seen as good and just. However, the ultimate value, the absolute reference of our European societies, is no longer freedom, but equality, that being true equality, the holy grail of socialism.

This socialization is a process that will not come to a natural end before communism, itself a deferred collapse.

To bring an end to this, we recommend endorsing a constitutional law, even supra-constitutional, prohibiting public authorities from allowing their public expenditure to exceed 40% of GDP.[10]

The calculation of this ratio should be undertaken each year by an independent body, such as the Court of Auditors, and no budget should be put to a vote without its prior validation.

The limitation of public expenditure and therefore of taxation will carry the weight of law, because socialization should cut both ways.

Step 5: Public expenditure should never exceed 40% of the annual wealth produced

---

[10] Why 40%? Like any threshold, that of 40% is somewhat arbitrary. Partly, because it is believed that by crossing the threshold of 40% of GDP the public expenditure of France began to get out of control, during the seven-year period of Giscard. Also, partly because public spending in countries such as Switzerland and the United States fluctuates between 35 and 40%, while these countries are at the top of most rankings of Western prosperity (IMF, World Bank, CIA World Factbook). The exact rate of the threshold is less important than the fact of its existence.

6. Accountability of the "magistrates"

On leaving office, the magistrates[11] of Athens and other Greek cities stood before the People's Court, which judged not only their possible corruption, but also their use of public funds. Should their efforts be considered to have been lacking, sentence was passed, ranging from the confiscation of property to death.

Different times, different customs. No one is eager to return to the severity of Greek law, which, in the less enlightened cities knew no other sanction than death.

Nevertheless, the idea of accountability deserves to be revitalized, in terms of debt.

Eighty years after John Maynard Keynes' masterpiece *The General Theory of Employment, Interest and Money* (1936), the balance of Keynesianism seems somewhat unstable. In practice, Keynesianism, particularly in the simplified form that we know today — *à la* The Financial Times — has only served to legitimize the increase in public spending by means of the debt.

Debt is an interesting phenomenon if considered in the light of moral philosophy. Debt is nothing else than a deferred tax, that is to say a tax on our children. People cherish their children. Paradoxically however, the debt — this tax on our children — is infinitely better accepted than tax on ourselves.

It is a fact. A sad fact maybe but very much a fact. Calling upon the pseudo-scientific backing of Keynesianism, debt growth has thus become a phenomenon parallel to the exponential development of taxation.

---

[11] In the most general sense i.e. that being any agent of the public service and not in the narrow sense of being a member of the judiciary.

In other words, our states are no longer content, to finance themselves, to tax the present generation, yet they must take a fraction of the wealth that has *not yet been produced* by future generations.

Since 1945, the growth of public debt in Western Europe has been linear. There are periods of remission, even fractional repayment of capital, but the norm is soon restored and it falls back into its arithmetic, even geometric, progression.

States such Italy and Belgium have had more than 100% public debt for decades — that is to say, a debt greater than all the wealth produced in one year! — and France has recently joined the front runners and is busy elbowing her way forward.

Such states must devote a significant portion of their tax revenues to the service of debt *interest* alone, thereby condemning themselves to financial servitude.

Except for war, nothing justifies debt, which is only the means for the politicians to buy support, to guarantee election.

Public debt should be made extraconstitutional, and the "magistrates" depository of public money be linked to their personal funds in case of debt at the end of their mandate.

Step 6: Any civil servant, who at the end of their role has engendered debt, will answer for it from their personal funds.[12]

---

[12] Nothing should prevent any lack of respect for this law being tried in the ordinary courts, including for the judiciary themselves.

7. Pluralism

It is a given that state propaganda requires the centralized control of information. As achieved by the Nazi *Propagandastaffel* service ... to name but one such institution. Yet, in reality, such is nothing but a primitive method of propaganda.

For we know today that other forms of propaganda are every bit as effective — and even more so, since they can be employed without suppression or apparent brutality.

Surveys show that in Western Europe as in the United States, 80% of journalists on average claim to be leftists. The Socialist Left, the Communist Left, the Islamophile Left, the Environmental-activist Left, ... but always the Left.

In other words, the overwhelming majority of journalists in the "traditional media" share essentially the same outlook, the same values, the same knee-jerk reflexes, the same conception of the state, the same expectations of those in power, the same ideas ... We speak in philosophy of *Weltanschauung*.

In such a context, there is no need to implement a centralized bureau of information: those in the press do so very well of their own accord, without any control required.

Centralized propaganda, diffuse propaganda: the result is the same.

The American case is enlightening. Indeed, from the narrow point of view of the French or Belgian Francophone, it is tempting to relate the *ideological monochromatism* of the traditional media to the public subsidy received. How, indeed, can one expect real independence from the state from a publicly-funded media?

Nevertheless, the American case reminds us that this monochromatism is no less significant in countries where there is no subsidization of the press. *The New York Times, The Washington Post*, CNN, NBC, ABC, ... an endless litany of outright left-wing bodies, whomsoever their owners and funding mechanisms be. 80% of Belgian journalists claim to be left-wing and 80% of American journalists claim the same. These are facts.

An antidote for this diffuse propaganda is the freedom of the Internet. On the Web, everyone is part of the media, and everyone has the opportunity to create a collective media. Thus, we see evermore in the United States and, to a lesser extent in Europe, new media, leaning very much to the Right (Drudge Report, FoxNews, Breitbart, Daily Caller, Gateway Pundit, etc.). This new-generation media has allowed a rebalancing of the information available without which the election of a Donald J. Trump to the presidency of the United States would probably never have been possible.

In countries where, like France and French-speaking Belgium, the government funds the media, there is another way to rebalance the public debate, nowadays so disproportionately skewed: the imposition of quotas.

Public broadcasters and the publicly-funded newspapers would be obliged to employ a minimum of 30% of journalists whose views are to the right, thus representative of the public at large.[13] Compliance with these quotas should be ensured by the threat of financial sanctions, or even the loss of public financing. There is no moral or rational reason to subsidize propaganda.

---

[13] In most Western countries, the proportion of citizens claiming to support the right or the left is largely equivalent.

In the United States, some of the judges and prosecutors are elected by the public, which ensures a real diversity of opinion within the judiciary. However, in countries such as France, where all the judges are appointed, it should be noted that in the end the overwhelming majority of judges claim left- and extreme left-wing affiliations and that an openly communist trade union has sneaked in and insulted with impunity litigants, judges, politicians, even relatives of victims (the *"mur des cons"*).

Therefore, it would be healthy either to elect at least some of the European judiciary — starting with the justices of the peace — or to impose ideological quotas, with a minimal representation of judges tending to the right.

How can there be any reason, be that ethical or rational, to employ only left-wing judges?

And then there are the universities. At the risk of seeming repetitive — the coincidence is disturbing — we find the same left-wing imperialism that is imposed in the media: in our universities — even the most prestigious — 80% of professors and academic staff claim to be left-wing.

Any university receiving public money — i.e. every university in Europe — and, more broadly, any publicly-funded school should guarantee a minimum of ideological diversity, or suffer having its public funding reduced or eliminated.

To sum this chapter up, after half a century of the implantation of like-minded personnel and out-and-out Trotskyite subversion, which has seen the left appropriating almost every unelected public office, it is time to restore the balance.

Step 7: Ensure effective ideological diversity in the press, education and the judiciary.

8. ECHR

Twenty-six percent of the voters who voted for Trump in the November the 8th, 2016 presidential election said they were primarily motivated by the fact that their president would have the ability to appoint one, perhaps two or three, new judges to the Supreme Court of the United States.[14]

Why is this noteworthy? Because this highlights, once again, the difference in political maturity between Americans and Europeans. While the former have understood, and perfectly integrated, that issues crucial to society should end up in the Supreme Court, the Europeans persist in seeing the judge as being unable to arbitrate over any political consideration.

It barely merits mentioning that herein there is no suggestion that the judicial function be purely political. But it would be equally absurd to deny its partially political character.

In America, the majority of the Supreme Court were leftist for no less than a *sixty-year period* (!), until the recent realignment with the appointment of Judge Roberts (2005). With the arrival of the two judges appointed by Trump — Gorsuch, Kavanaugh — the majority of the Supreme Court is now demonstrably rightist for the first time since Franklin D. Roosevelt.

In Europe, the Right denied, until recently, the political dimension of the judicial function, which lead to two supreme jurisdictions — the Court of Justice of the European Union (CJEU) and the European Court of Human Rights (ECHR) — being

---

[14] "A quarter of Republicans voted for Trump to get Supreme Court picks — and it paid off", *The Washington Post*, https://www.washingtonpost.com/news/politics/wp/2018/06/26/a-quarter-of-republicans-voted-for-trump-to-get-supreme-court-picks-and-it-paid-off/

overwhelmingly composed of left-wing and extreme left-wing judges, many of whom have been funded by George Soros's foundations.[15]

An evident shift that we owe to the combined effect of leftist cronyism and the unfathomable naïveté of the right in Western Europe.

The CJEU and ECHR possess between them a power comparable to that of the Supreme Court of the United States. But as the CJEU is inextricably linked to that of the future of the EU as a whole, we will not deal with it here.

As for the ECHR, technically there is a way, for a State, to escape from under the deadweight of its case law, for example in the field of migration: to exit the ECHR (its convention) then re-adhere with certain conditions imposed. However, it would have to jump from the pan into the fire; leaving an extreme jurisprudence only to be roasted by ten others.

In truth, the balance sheet of the ECHR can only be described as delusional. Unelected judges have surreptitiously substituted the concept of *universal man*, dear to French revolutionaries, for the Burkean conception of human rights in Europe as outlined in the 1950 Convention.

Thus we saw this court, under the impetus of among others the Belgian judge Françoise Tulkens — to name but one — adopt in 2012 the infamous Hirsi judgment, which condemned the return of clandestine immigrants, intercepted in the Mediterranean, to

---

[15] One example: in 2018, two of Albania's three candidates for the post of judge at the ECHR worked for the Open Society of George Soros: https://www.valeursactuelles.com/ Company / shadow-of-george-soros-flat-on-the-appointment-of-new-judges-of-the-court- European-of-rights-of-the man-99634

their point of origin. This judgment marked the beginning of what is wrongly presented by the left as a migratory "crisis" befalling Europe like a natural disaster.

It is not so. This migration crisis is entirely of our own making, it is the offspring of the extremism of the ECHR, which in turn is possible only because of the political monochromatism of its judges.

Until the Hirsi judgement, a migrant who took to the sea did it with the intention of *not* being caught, to quietly enter Europe and to get lost in the mass of illegal immigrants. To do this, he paid the services of people traffickers well versed in crossing the Mediterranean.

Since the Hirsi decision, all is changed: the clandestine takes to the sea with the express intention of being intercepted — by a Frontex boat, or a boat chartered by an NGO — because he knows that that ship will have the "jurisprudential" obligation to escort him or her into European territory!

This ruling thus had four direct consequences. One, the exponential growth of those taking to the water. Two, a fortune for the mafia smuggling networks whose turnover is today comparable to the drug trade. Three, left wing NGOs have ships at sea with the express intention of serving as a "ferry service" between the African coast and the ports of Europe. The fourth is the thousands of children, men and women who perish now every year in the Mediterranean.

In principle, the ruling is absurd. In its effects, it is criminal.

The ECHR cannot be saved, and the same must be said for its delusional jurisprudence. Any state wishing to regain its sovereignty, on issues as fundamental as the control of its borders, has no choice but to withdraw from the ECHR.

Step 8: Any state wishing to regain sovereignty over issues such as border control will have to withdraw from the ECHR.

9. Maghreb

The solution to the migration problem — one of the two key elements of this text, the other being the socialization of Europe by the Law and taxation — presupposes the full collaboration of the Maghreb countries, through which pass or from which come the overwhelming majority entering Europe illegally.

European liberal guilt over colonization dictates international relations, and occludes a simple fact: without the help of Europe, the Maghreb will rapidly succumb to economic collapse.

Europe is the recipient of 60% of all North Africa's exports. Eighty percent of investment in the Maghreb is European. Ninety percent of remittances to the Maghreb come from Europe. Eighty to ninety percent of the income from tourism in countries such as Morocco or Tunisia comes from European.

Thus, it is evident that if Europe suspends economic cooperation with these countries, their economies will collapse.

Therefore, those in Europe who say that *unfortunately* North Africa does not want to host "hotspots" and that *unfortunately* some of these countries do not want to welcome back their clandestine migrants and that *unfortunately* the migration crisis is thus unstoppable, are at best wrong. Cutting to the chase, these countries have everything to gain from vigorous and frank collaboration with Europe.

Let's draw a comparison. When, during the 2016 election campaign, candidate Trump stated that Mexico, Canada, the EU and China would have no choice but to cooperate, he was derided. What? You are going to force a country to collaborate? If it refuses, what will you do, declare war?!

The logic of that particular presidential candidate was, in reality, pragmatic: a country which has a trade surplus with the States – that is to say, it sells more to the US than the US does to it – has two choices: either collaborate, or impoverish itself (this impoverishment can cause, in the case of Mexico and China, outright collapse).

The same is true, for different but similar reasons, of the Maghreb countries. Europe is propping up their economies. Vigorous and complete cooperation is the only choice, especially regarding the illegal immigrants issuing from their countries!

Europe must realise its position and power, which is economically and militarily real.

Step 9: Index all forms of economic interaction with the Maghreb countries to their full collaboration regarding migration.

10. Civilization

We must not allow ourselves to be trapped in false debates such as the "The Clash of Civilizations" or the objective "superiority" of a particular society, so often put in terms too general for the proposition to be countered.

The idea that no civilization can claim objective superiority is not without merit. There is, in fact, no objective criteria for assessing the relative worth of Western, Chinese, the Islamic (wrongly entitled Arab-Muslim) or Hindu civilizations.

Let's refine the debate: in terms existential and societal, humanity has made little progress since the Greeks. Is man a more moral or perfect creature than he was at the time of Solon or Cicero? This seems doubtful. Are our institutions more efficient than those of the Greeks or Romans? We may labour under certain illusions but if one seriously studies Law and the ancient institutions, one finds that even the separation of power — which eludes our institutions — was fully theorized and practiced in ancient Athens and Rome.

In reality, there is only one area in which humanity is progressing: technology, and the science that underpins it. Here the progress, so very *human,* seems giddy, Promethean, exponential and inexhaustible.

Simple optical illusion! For, the apparent normalcy of these advances, which makes them appear consubstantial to human development, should not make us forget that during most of its evolution, humanity did not accomplish any such advances and that, according to the French adage, it took as long for Napoleon to get to Egypt as it took the Romans to get there.

These technological marvels achieve the most beautiful, the most noble conquest of the human mind, promising us limitless horizons, the entire universe our playground. Now, these technological and scientific advances are by and large indivisible from Western civilization[16]. If we do recognise the magnificence of these accomplishments, then likewise we must recognise the precedence of Western civilization.

The term "Western civilization" is quite abstract. What are the driving forces of this civilization? Why have these advances stemmed from and have been possible, disseminated and "institutionalized" only in the fecundity of the West?

There are as many answers to this question as there are thinkers who are interested in it. Let's try to find the firm ground of certainty in that quagmire of conjecture.

---

[16] Most countries now contribute, to varying degrees, thanks to the globalization of trade. China contributes to technological progress as much as Europe. Nevertheless, the system that has become globalized is as Western in its source as it is in its institutions: freedom of enterprise, the free market, research and development.

10. Civilization

Three institutions emerge, inseparable from the history of the West and without which no real ongoing technical progress could be achieved: freedom, the market, the rule of law.

Should Man be bound to a Law that is claimed to be divine, his freedom will be of a restricted nature and hindered in its application. The question is not that a Law allows or prohibits technical progress in particular; it is that freedom be the underlying principle of the whole moral, legal and political structure.

The comparison with Islam does bear fruit. The Islamic civilization successfully colonized a significant fraction of the neighbouring areas of the basin from which it originated, and beyond. This ultimately brought about the crusades which brought into the field European and Islamic armies of comparable strength.

However it was not until many years after the crusades that, despite the bravery of its armies, the forces of Islam suffered a lasting defeat due to the emerging technical superiority of European weaponry. These weapons were not God-given but arose from an improbable civilizational crucible, in many ways barbaric, primitive, bloodthirsty, politically authoritarian. But fundamentally free, liberated from a divine castrator's logos and consecrating *de facto* if not *de jure* the freedom to conceive, to invent, to undertake, to manufacture — to be.

This ontological freedom is both the specificity of Western civilization, and its main catalyst.

Next let's consider the market. Technical progress is conceivable in any context; society, culture or civilization: it suffices for a gifted individual, or a hardworking, ingenious and inquisitive person, to actuate ideas, drawings and prototypes to generate the potential of technical progress.

But without the market, in isolation, it will not achieve that potential. It is the market, thanks to the promise and actual generation of wealth, that allows and encourages the actuation of an innovation; which will in turn be taken on by a manufacturer or company as part of a larger project, all virtually infinite, creative and, self-perpetuating.

As a *continuous process,* technological progress is conceivable only in the context of a market economy, whose actors freely fix the price of components and products marketed. Without price freedom[17], and the same goes for information, there is no market. The market is the *institutionalization* of technical progress.

The third historical specificity of Western civilization is the rule of law, that is to say the limitation of the arbitrary use of power. When the individual is reliant on goodwill yet subjected to the violence of the Minotaur, according to Jouvenel's metaphor, he/she becomes a cog, a number, a variable, by default a *res nullius*, losing motivation to go beyond subsistence. The legal security of the individual and of trade is the *sine qua non* of freedom and of a relatively peaceful and efficient market economy.

Freedom, the market and the rule of law form the ontological triptych of our civilization. We must rediscover this truth and teach it.

---

[17] This is not the hackneyed myth of "pure and perfect competition", that bugbear of logic drawn upon by left-wing economists in a dusty corner of liberal theoretical thought, whose worth is doubtful, even and especially as an "ideal" representation. Nothing that is human is perfect and if we had to wait until freedom was pure and perfect for capitalism to develop, we would still be busy hunting and gathering. Ideas of purity and perfection are *radically foreign* to the concepts of real freedom and the market in practice. The freedom in question here is always relative, imperfect, constrained. That it asserts itself in the background with all the force of a paradigm, a reference, a recourse, a *habitus* — will be enough to ensure its spread.

Step 10: Understand, acknowledge and teach the driving forces of Western civilization.

Conclusion:
Ten steps to reclaim Europe

History would be unfathomably convoluted if we had lived through as many "turning points" as the intellectuals claim.

The challenges of our time are hardly distinguishable, neither in nature nor difficulty, from previous eras.

Many scholars want us to believe that Man's history — there is no other — is governed by external forces. This notion is often expressed in one of two ways.

The first is too general to be refutable; it is outside the field of rational discussion. Consider Hegelian determinism[18] and Marxian materialism[19].

The second is refutable and, has always been, immediately refuted. Consider the cyclic determinisms[20] of the Greek writers to the present day.

The history of each period is shaped by the minds of that time. To submit to the "forces" of history means to submit to the ideas and will of others.

---

[18] The idea that historical progress is rational in its own right.

[19] The idea that historical progress is the fruit of the "agonism" of divergent material interests, finally resulting in a classless and stateless society.

[20] That is, the theory that one constitutional form will necessarily evolve into another form, and so on.

The European right is thus confronted with a simple choice: to regain control of historical progress or to persist in its effective submission to the ideas and categorization of the egalitarian left.